Grassland Biome

by Grace Hansen

Abdo
BIOMES
Kids

abdopublishing.com

Published by Abdo Kids, a division of ABDO, PO Box 398166, Minneapolis, Minnesota 55439.

Copyright © 2017 by Abdo Consulting Group, Inc. International copyrights reserved in all countries. No part of this book may be reproduced in any form without written permission from the publisher.

Printed in the United States of America, North Mankato, Minnesota.

052016

092016

 THIS BOOK CONTAINS RECYCLED MATERIALS

Photo Credits: iStock, Minden Pictures, Shutterstock

Production Contributors: Teddy Borth, Jennie Forsberg, Grace Hansen

Design Contributors: Laura Mitchell, Dorothy Toth

Cataloging-in-Publication Data

Names: Hansen, Grace, author.

Title: Grassland biome / by Grace Hansen.

Description: Minneapolis, MN : Abdo Kids, [2017] | Series: Biomes |
    Includes bibliographical references and index.

Identifiers: LCCN 2015959103 | ISBN 9781680805031 (lib. bdg.) |
    ISBN 9781680805598 (ebook) | ISBN 9781680806151 (Read-to-me ebook)

Subjects: LCSH: Grassland ecology--Juvenile literature.

Classification: DDC 577.4--dc23

LC record available at http://lccn.loc.gov/2015959103

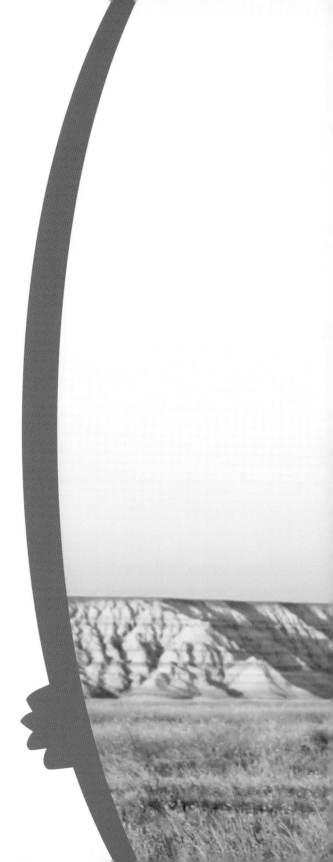

Table of Contents

What is a Biome?

A biome is a large area. It has certain plants and animals. It also has a certain climate.

desert

forest

4

freshwater

marine

grassland

tundra

5

Grassland Biomes

Grasslands are biomes.

There are two main grasslands.

Tropical grasslands are near

the **equator**. They are also

called savannas.

Savannas are warm all
year long. They have
wet and dry seasons.

9

Temperate grasslands are further from the **equator**. Many are in the middle of continents. Some are near oceans. Winters are cold and summers are hot.

11

Plants

Short and tall grasses cover grasslands. Small shrubs can grow, too. There are very few trees.

12

13

Temperate grasslands have wild flowers. Its grasses are often short. **Grazing** animals keep grasses short.

15

Animals

Bison **graze** in prairies. Wild horses and deer graze, too.

17

Savannas are home to many animals. Wombats live in Australian savannas. Kangaroos and other animals live there, too.

African savannas are home to zebras and wildebeests. Lions and lots of other animals live there, too.

Things You Might See in a Grassland Biome

temperate

tropical

bison

gazelle

prairie dog

vulture

coneflower

umbrella thorn acacia

22

Glossary

climate – weather conditions that are usual in an area over a long period of time.

equator – imaginary line drawn around the Earth that divides it into the northern and southern hemispheres.

graze – to feed on growing grasses and herbage.

Index

abdokids.com

Use this code to log on to abdokids.com and access crafts, games, videos, and more!

Abdo Kids Code:
BGK5031